A Christmas STOCKING

A Child Is Born In Bethlehem

Mary was a pure and humble maiden, and Joseph was a good and honest man. They lived in Nazareth, a city in Galilee. God loved Mary and Joseph for their goodness and made a special plan for them.

One day, while Mary was alone at home, the angel Gabriel appeared before her. Mary was frightened at first, but Gabriel said, "Do not be afraid, for the Lord thinks highly of you. You shall be the mother of the Lord's son. The Child will be great, and his name will be 'Jesus.'"

Shortly after that, Mary and Joseph were married. It was then that Mary told Joseph that the angel Gabriel had told her that she would be the mother of the son of God. At first, Joseph did not believe it. But that night, the angel of the Lord came and told Joseph that it was true: Mary was to deliver the son of God and Joseph was to be the Child's father. Now Mary and Joseph could be glad together.

Months passed, and the time for the Child to be born was near. At the same time, the mean and greedy Roman ruler, Caesar Augustus, made a law that forced every man in Judea to return immediately to the place where he had been born. There, the people were to register their names and property, so that the ruler could collect money from them. Because Joseph had been born in Bethlehem, he and Mary were ordered to go there.

The journey from Nazareth to Bethlehem was long and hard. Joseph walked on foot, leading Mary on their donkey. After several days, they came to Bethlehem ... at an inn where they hoped ... ight. "I'm sorry," said the

WHA

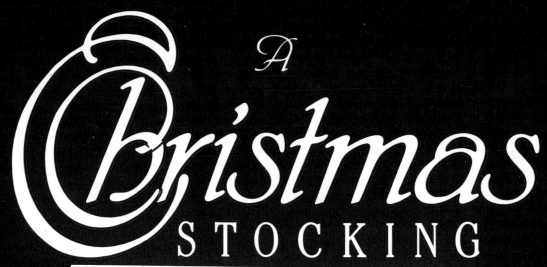

A Child's Treasury For The Festive Season

Louise Betts Egan

LINE ILLUSTRATIONS BY KENNETH SPENGLER

SIMON & SCHUSTER

London • Sydney • New York • Tokyo • Toronto

THE FIRST

The Prophecy

Long, long ago, God looked down from Heaven and saw that His world was filled with trouble. People fought each other; some people were sick; others were poor and never had enough to eat. God saw that not enough people were obeying His laws. He decided to create a son, a man who would not only help save the world from misery, but add to its glory.

"I will call my son, 'Jesus,' " God told the angels in Heaven. This name means, "God saves."

Then, God went down to earth and whispered His plan to a good and honest

The Shepherds Hear The News

On the night that Jesus was born there were shepherds in a nearby field keeping watch over their flocks. Suddenly, the sky filled with light. The angel of the Lord appeared and the shepherds trembled in fear.

"Don't be afraid," said the angel, "for I have great news. Today, in the city of Bethlehem, a Child was born who is Christ the King. You shall find this Child wrapped in swaddling clothes, lying in a manger."

When the angel finished speaking, a multitude of angels appeared in the sky. "Glory to God in the highest!" they sang. "Peace on earth and good will toward men!"

After the angels had gone, the shepherds hurried to Bethlehem. There, they found Mary and Joseph sitting near the Baby Jesus, who was lying in the manger.

"An angel told us about the newborn King," said the shepherds. "May we see Him?"

Mary smiled and nodded. Joseph led the shepherds to the manger. They bowed down and thanked God for sending them the Saviour, who would bring joy and hope into their lives.

A Child Is Born In Bethlehem

Mary was a pure and humble maiden, and Joseph was a good and honest man. They lived in Nazareth, a city in Galilee. God loved Mary and Joseph for their goodness and made a special plan for them.

One day, while Mary was alone at home, the angel Gabriel appeared before her. Mary was frightened at first, but Gabriel said, "Do not be afraid, for the Lord thinks highly of you. You shall be the mother of the Lord's son. The Child will be great, and his name will be 'Jesus.' "

Shortly after that, Mary and Joseph were married. It was then that Mary told Joseph that the angel Gabriel had told her that she would be the mother of the son of God. At first, Joseph did not believe it. But that night, the angel of the Lord came and told Joseph that it was true: Mary was to deliver the son of God and Joseph was to be the Child's father. Now Mary and Joseph could be glad together.

Months passed, and the time for the Child to be born was near. At the same time, the mean and greedy Roman ruler, Caesar Augustus, made a law that forced every man in Judea to return immediately to the place where he had been born. There, the people were to register their names and property, so that the ruler could collect money from them. Because Joseph had been born in Bethlehem, he and Mary were ordered to go there.

The journey from Nazareth to Bethlehem was long and hard. Joseph walked on foot, leading Mary on their donkey. After several days, they came to Bethlehem and stopped at an inn where they hoped to spend the night. "I'm sorry," said the owner, "but there's no room at the inn."

Mary and Joseph turned away, but the man saw that Mary was going to have a baby and he offered to help. "You can stay in the stable," he suggested. Mary and Joseph were grateful for any shelter, and the stable was warm and dry.

That night, which we now call Christmas Eve, Mary gave birth to a little baby boy. To keep him warm, she wrapped him tightly in strips of linen. Joseph made a cradle for the Child by spreading clean hay in the box from which the sheep ate.

Mary and Joseph were filled with joy and wonder. Jesus Christ the Saviour had been born!

North Wind Picture Archives

The Shepherds Hear The News

On the night that Jesus was born there were shepherds in a nearby field keeping watch over their flocks. Suddenly, the sky filled with light. The angel of the Lord appeared and the shepherds trembled in fear.

"Don't be afraid," said the angel, "for I have great news. Today, in the city of Bethlehem, a Child was born who is Christ the King. You shall find this Child wrapped in swaddling clothes, lying in a manger."

When the angel finished speaking, a multitude of angels appeared in the sky. "Glory to God in the highest!" they sang. "Peace on earth and good will toward men!"

After the angels had gone, the shepherds hurried to Bethlehem. There, they found Mary and Joseph sitting near the Baby Jesus, who was lying in the manger.

"An angel told us about the newborn King," said the shepherds. "May we see Him?"

Mary smiled and nodded. Joseph led the shepherds to the manger. They bowed down and thanked God for sending them the Saviour, who would bring joy and hope into their lives.

The Three Wise Men

Far away in the East three wise men gazed at a strange star in the night sky. These men, who are also known as the three kings or "Magi," had never seen this star before and marveled at how much brighter it was than all the other stars.

"It must have special meaning," said one wise man.

"Perhaps it is a sign from God," said another.

The third wise man, thinking of the prophecy of Isaiah, said, "Maybe it is God's sign that our Saviour has been born."

Later that night, the wise men set out on camels and rode across the desert toward the bright star. Eventually, they came to Jerusalem, where they stopped at the palace of Herod, King of Judea.

"Where can we find the newborn Baby who will be our new King?" they asked Herod. "We have seen his star in the east and have come to worship him."

King Herod had not heard anything at all about the Baby Jesus, and was troubled by the news. He called together his chief priests and scribes and asked where this Child was born.

"The prophet said that the Child will be born in Bethlehem," they replied.

King Herod then told the three wise men to continue on their way and to come back and tell him when they had found the Christ Child. "Then I can go and worship him, too," said King Herod. But the king did not mean what he said.

What the wise men did not know was that King Herod was an evil man and jealous of anyone more powerful than he. It worried him when the wise men and priests said that a new "king" had been born. King Herod wanted to be the only king in the land.

North Wind Picture Archives

The three wise men left the palace and continued following the star, which shone brightly over Bethlehem. The star led them right to Mary, Joseph, and the Baby Jesus. When they saw Jesus, the wise men fell to their knees in worship. They then opened the treasure boxes they had brought the Christ Child. Inside were gifts of gold, and frankincense and myrrh, which were precious perfumes.

The wise men were happy to have seen the Baby Jesus and looked forward to telling King Herod that they had found him. But that night, they each had a dream that warned them against telling King Herod, for fear that he would harm Jesus. The next day, the three wise men headed back to their land by another way, instead of going through Jerusalem to tell King Herod.

Jesus was safe. He would grow up and teach others to spread the word of God to as many people as possible. And the message of Jesus continues today.

Robert Gray

KEEPING THE SPIRIT OF CHRISTMAS TODAY

The Christmas spirit is what makes you feel good when you do something nice for someone. The Christmas spirit helps you feel happy on an ordinary day. That same spirit settles fights between enemies and turns misfortunes into blessings.

The Christmas spirit is something to keep inside you all year round, not just during the month of December. People refresh and renew this spirit on Christmas Day and the weeks surrounding it by continuing customs and family traditions that have been passed on through the years. Here are some of the things people do:

• **Place a fairy, an angel, or a star on top of the Christmas tree.** The fairy or angel remind people of the angel Gabriel who told Mary she would be the mother of God's son, and the angel who told the shepherds the news of Jesus' birth. The star reminds people of the star of Bethlehem that led the three wise men to Jesus.

• **Sing Christmas carols.** A "carol" is a joyous song, especially about Christmas. Many of the older carols, like *Away In A Manger, The First Noël,* and *We Three Kings* tell about the birth of Christ. In a way, they are Christmas stories set to music. Other carols, like *Deck the Halls* and *We Wish You A Merry Christmas* bring out the more festive mood of Christmas, which makes the season extra busy and happy.

Around Christmas time, carols are sung in many places besides church. They are often sung in school, as well as played in shops and on the radio and television.

It's fun to go "Christmas caroling." Groups of friends both large and small can often be heard singing carols from house to house in the evenings. Sometimes caroling groups bring a special cheer by singing at nursing homes and hospitals.

• **Set Up A Crèche.** A "crèche," an old French word meaning "crib" or "manger," is a model of the Nativity scene, reminding people of the night Jesus was born. Inside a model stable are the figures of Mary and Joseph looking at the Baby Jesus lying in the manger. They are usually surrounded by figures of the shepherds and their sheep, and the three wise men with their camels.

In some towns, large crèches are put up in the middle of town. Many people also have small crèches in their homes.

Robert Gray

Robert Gray

Tony Cenicola

● **Exchange Gifts With Friends and Family.** Though people gave each other gifts long before Christ was born, giving and receiving presents at Christmas is a reminder of the gifts the three wise men and others gave Jesus. Giving gifts is also a way to feel the Christmas spirit, because you are doing something nice for someone else.

● **Give Money or Gifts To Others In Need.** During the holiday season, many collections are taken up for different people: for the poor, the sick, and the hungry. You may also hear or read about other needy people: perhaps a family's house has burned down, and they need clothes and shelter.

To help distribute money and gifts to these people, newspapers often have special charity funds. In many cities, members of the Salvation Army or other charities stand on street corners, ringing bells and sometimes playing hymns with horns and trumpets, encouraging passers-by to give money to the poor. Schools and offices often take up collections of toys to give to poor children. Hospitals also collect toys to give to sick children who can't be home for Christmas.

In Great Britain, Australia, and Canada, December 26 is called "Boxing Day." This is traditionally the day when people give gifts or money to employees and servants. The day is named after the little clay boxes in which the money was given in medieval days. Later, wealthy people used to put their Christmas feast leftovers in boxes and give them to their servants.

Robert Gray

• **Go To Church On Christmas Eve or Christmas Day.** For many people, going to church on those days helps bring the meaning of Christmas right to the heart. Christmas carols are sung. The chapters in the Bible describing the Nativity are read, and sometimes children put on a pageant that also recalls the night Jesus was born. Many churches are decorated with candles and wreaths. The church choirs, which usually have been practising for weeks, can sound magical at a Christmas service. For many, church is the one quiet moment among a flurry of holiday activities when it's possible to remember most clearly what Christmas is all about.

Robert Gray

CHRISTMAS GREENS

Before There Was Christmas

Thousands of years ago, and long before Christ was born, people did not understand what caused winter. Winter frightened them. They believed that the gods who watched over the crops and harvests during the spring, summer, and autumn had suddenly departed. Without these gods, there would be no more food. The gods' disappearance seemed to explain why plants died and trees grew bare; why the grass turned brown and the ground froze; and why the wind turned sharp and icy.

Daylight grew shorter and shorter, especially in Northern Europe, where snow also fell thick and deep. The fear that the sun might not return made people nervous and unhappy.

To cheer themselves up and to encourage the gods to return to earth, people all over Europe held huge festivals at the end of December. These festivals were times of great merrymaking for all. There were enormous feasts and bonfires. Houses and festival halls were decorated in evergreen branches, holly, and ivy.

Keith Glasgow

© Roz Joseph/Omni-Photo Communications

Evergreen Magic

In those ancient times, any plant that stayed green during the cold winter was thought to have magical powers. For that reason, people sometimes wore crowns of ivy and laurel around their heads. Others would drape the vines about their homes. People also would gather branches of fir, spruce, pine, and hemlock from the large evergreen forests and decorate their homes with them. The sight of all this greenery gave people hope that the other seasons would soon return. These traditions are still carried on during the Christmas holidays today, but mostly because they add to the wonderful and fun spirit of the season.

Mistletoe

This Christmas plant, which grows on a vine, was once thought to have special healing powers. It has thickly clustered leaves and tiny, white berries. People thought mistletoe was magic because its vine did not grow up from the ground. Instead, it seemed to start from nowhere and just wrap itself around tree trunks and branches.

What these people did not know was that birds ate the mistletoe berries and would then spit out the seeds. The seeds would fall into the tree bark and plant themselves there.

Ancient, mystical priests called "druids" would dress in long, hooded robes and go into the forests to cut the magical mistletoe for their religious ceremonies. They took great care to make sure the plant never touched the ground. If it did, the druids believed the mistletoe would lose its magic.

Today, mistletoe is hung from the ceilings in many homes in Great Britain and North America during the Christmas season. Any young girl or woman who stands beneath it is supposed to receive a kiss. This custom began with the ancient pagan Britons, who hung a sprig of mistletoe above their doors to scare away witches. Anyone who entered the doorway was quickly given a kiss.

When Christianity came to Great Britain, the church did not accept any of the pagan beliefs attached to the mistletoe. Though other evergreens were acceptable, mistletoe was not.

At Christmas time today, churches often light advent wreaths and decorate with evergreen branches. But if you look for mistletoe, you probably won't find it.

A gatherer brings mistletoe to market.

The Poinsettia

The Mexicans first called this plant, "Flower of the Holy Night," because of the way its green leaves mysteriously turn red in December. The poinsettia has come to symbolize Christmas for many people in other parts of the world.

There is a legend that tells of a little Mexican boy who wished to give a gift to the Christ Child. But the boy was poor and had no gift to give Him. One Christmas Eve, he stood outside the church. The little boy was too ashamed to go inside with nothing to offer.

"At least I can pray," the boy thought to himself. When he said, "Amen," to his amazement, a beautiful plant had grown where he knelt. The plant had flaming red leaves arranged like a star, and a lovely yellow blossom shone like a light in the centre.

The little boy realized that this flower was a gift from God. He gently plucked it and then carried it into the church and proudly laid his gift at the altar.

Robert Gray

Brilliant poinsettias seem to shout out "Happy Christmas!"

Holly

Like mistletoe, holly was once believed to have special magical powers that frightened off witches and other evil spirits. In Great Britain the druids wore a sprig of holly on their robes whenever they went into the forest to cut some mistletoe. They believed the holly protected them from evil spirits. Such spirits could force them to drop the mistletoe onto the ground and destroy the plant's powers.

In the same way, unmarried women in ancient Britain attached bits of holly to their beds. They hoped that the holly would ward off ghosts and devils.

Holly plays a special role in Christmas celebrations in Great Britain. Indeed, holly is so well-loved that it is mentioned in British carols, such as "Deck the Halls with Boughs of Holly." There's even a carol all about holly called "The Holly and the Ivy." Holly is used for decorating homes at Christmas time, and people use it to make garlands.

It is said that the crown of thorns that Jesus wore was made of holly. At that time, holly berries were white. But as the prickly crown pressed deeply into Jesus' forehead, his blood stained the berries. From then on, holly berries have remained red as a reminder of Jesus' suffering for all people.

The Christmas Tree Tradition

Today Christmas trees adorn homes all over the world during the month of December. To many, these decorated evergreen trees represent the spirit of Christmas. To others, they represent the continuation of life in the winter.

People first wrote about Christmas trees about five hundred years ago, in Germany. There, it is said, a religious man named Martin Luther was walking through the woods one starry night around Christmas time. He was so struck by the beauty of the starlight on the evergreen trees that he chopped a small tree down and brought it home for his wife and children. He lighted the tree with small candles, which he said represented Christ as the Light of the World.

The idea of Christmas trees began to spread throughout Northern Europe, where evergreen trees grow tall and strong. Even so, the first Christmas trees—like Martin Luther's—were small enough to display on a table. Family members would put their gifts on the table underneath the little tree. The trees were decorated with bright paper roses,

glass ornaments, apples, biscuits, and sweets. Small lighted candles were then carefully placed at the ends of the branches. (A pan of water was usually kept nearby, in case one of the candles accidentally dropped onto a branch.)

Christmas trees became popular in Great Britain in the nineteenth century. Prince Albert, the husband of Queen Victoria, loved them particularly, and the Queen and Prince put up the first British tree in 1841. The tree was at Windsor Castle, and was decorated with candles, sweets, biscuits, and fruits.

Christmas trees quickly became a tradition in Victorian homes. People grew more and more imaginative with their decorations, creating miniature furniture, instruments and dolls to hang on their trees. And, of course, they also added biscuits, sweets, and fruits.

When Germans went to the United States in the 1800s, they took the Christmas tree tradition with them. Other early Americans liked this tradition and quickly adopted it. No longer were Christmas trees small enough for tables. They would go out to the forest and chop down the tallest, most magnificent tree they saw.

Tree-decorating Advice

Today many families decorate their Christmas trees with both handmade and shop-bought ornaments. Sometimes people collect ornaments on holidays. Over the years, many ornaments begin to mean something special to each family. Taking the pretty decorations out of their boxes often gives people a warm, good feeling. It adds to the joy of seeing the family tree decorated to its very best.

Sometimes people disagree about which ornament would look best where. Because decorating the tree is a shared activity, it's best to listen to one another's ideas; keep in mind that your tree will look good wherever you put the ornament.

However, it's best to put delicate ornaments high up, on strong branches where they are least likely to get knocked off. You may need to use a stepladder, so make sure an adult is watching you.

The lower branches are the ones people and pets bump into most often. For that reason, sturdy, unbreakable ornaments should go on the lower branches. That way, if an ornament does get knocked off, it won't break.

The Christmas tree at Rockefeller Center in New York City enchants all who come to see it. Nearby, on Fifth Avenue (right), holiday lights sparkle, invoking the spirit of the season.

Favourite Christmas Trees

Many large cities are known for their giant Christmas trees. These trees are visited by thousands of children and adults every year.

Some of these trees are made up of hundreds of normal-sized Christmas trees that have been tied together to make them several stories high. They are then covered in brilliant lights and ornaments. One such "tree" is in Chicago, U.S.A., inside Marshall Field's department store. It attracts many hundreds of children and adults each year.

Other cities put up a single, but larger than average, Christmas tree. In London, a giant tree stands in Trafalgar Square. The Norwegians send this tree every year, to thank the British for their help to Norway during World War II. Washington, D.C.'s Christmas tree, located near the White House, is decorated with fifty large, brightly coloured balls that represent each state. Another enormous tree is in New York City, at Rockefeller Center, where it towers over an outdoor skating rink.

Of course, the large and famous Christmas trees may not be everyone's favourite. Sometimes, the Christmas tree that lights up your own town square may seem to be the most beautiful tree of all.

Robert Gray

CHRISTMAS LIGHTS

At Christmas time, lights seem to go up everywhere. Whole streets are lined with small white or coloured lights that glisten like fairies. Strings of coloured lights brighten shopfronts, and cheery Christmas tree lights glow from inside homes.

Lights have long been a part of the Christmas tradition. The bright light from the Star of Bethlehem guided the three wise men to the Baby Jesus. Later, Jesus said to the Twelve Apostles, "Let your light so shine before men." He called these apostles "the light of the world."

The "light" Jesus meant was a spiritual one. He wanted his disciples to do their very best and to be an example to others. To this day, Christmas is a time when people remember those words through giving presents, good behaviour, and acts of kindness.

Churches light candles to recall the light that came to the world with the birth of Jesus Christ. The Advent wreath is one way of representing the spirit of

Christmas: Four candles are placed around a wreath and a new candle is lit each of the four Sundays of the Advent season, prior to Christmas day. On Christmas Eve, churches also hold special candlelight services.

A custom in many British homes is to place a candle in the window to light the way for the Christ Child's coming each December 25.

In the American Southwest, "luminarias," or Christmas lanterns, are a popular tradition. These lanterns are made by setting a small candle in a paper bag that is weighted down with moist sand. Sometimes whole neighbourhoods mark their driveways with luminarias, and the sight of hundreds of these glowing lanterns is splendid.

December is the coldest and darkest month of the year for many countries that celebrate Christmas. For that reason, lights are all the more important in adding cheer and warmth throughout the holidays.

Colour and lights create a special kind of magic at Christmas. The Lucia Queen (right), with a candle wreath on top of her head, brings a special Christmas breakfast to her family.

New York Public Library/Picture Collection

Customs With Candles—Caution!

Never attempt to make your own Christmas decoration that involves lighting candles or matches, unless you have *an adult's permission*. These decorations are beautiful when lit, but they can also be *dangerous* if the candle happens to fall over and catch fire. For that reason, it's important for an adult to supervise any candle-lighting.

St. Lucia Day—The Swedish Tribute to Light

Sweden's "Lucia Festival," on December 13, is held at a time when darkness falls in that country by mid-afternoon. The name Lucia, or Lucy, means "light," which is something Swedes especially treasure during the long winter nights.

The real Lucia was a kind and courageous Christian woman who lived in Italy in the fourth century. It is said that on the night before her wedding, Lucia gave all her money to the poor. Because no one could understand why she did that, Lucia was accused of being a witch and was burned at the stake on December 13 in the year 304. Even after her death, however, Lucia was said to continue helping those in need. For that reason, she was eventually made a saint.

When Christianity came to Sweden, St.

Lucia's role was combined with that of Berchta, the early goddess of the hearth, or fireplace. This goddess was loved for her good heart and for the special care she was said to give to children.

According to Swedish tradition, the oldest daughter of the family pretends to be St. Lucia on the morning of December 13. The "Lucia Queen" dresses in a long white gown and wears a special crown of evergreen boughs and four lighted candles upon her head. She rises before dawn to prepare coffee and special saffron buns and then serves them to the rest of the family, while they are still in bed.

As she goes from room to room, the Lucia Queen sings a song of promise that the darkness will end soon. The sight of this Lucia Queen, with the candles burning brightly on her evergreen crown, is one that brings hope, light, and happiness to all.

Robert Gray

SPECIAL CHRISTMAS WORDS

Advent is a season during the church year that begins on the last Sunday in November and ends on Christmas. "Advent" means "the coming of Jesus Christ." For many people, Advent is the time for improving one's thoughts and behaviour, in preparation for Christmas. The colour purple symbolizes Advent and you may notice its use in church during those weeks. Advent calendars and Advent wreaths are both good and fun ways to mark the coming of Christmas.

Christmas Seals. By the early 1900s Christmas cards had become popular and tons of Christmas mail overwhelmed post offices around the world. About that time, a young postal clerk in Denmark named Einar Holboell thought of using Christmas cards as a way to raise money for a good cause. He wanted to help the many people, especially children, who at that time were suffering and dying from the crippling disease tuberculosis.

Holboell looked at the hundreds of thousands of letters, parcels, and Christmas cards that swamped his post office. He thought that if each piece of mail carried an extra stamp that cost only a penny, the money could go toward building more hospitals and to treating tuberculosis.

Holboell talked about this idea to everyone he met and found that people were interested. Finally, even the Danish King Christian expressed his approval.

The first Christmas seal stamp came out in Denmark in 1904 and four million were sold. A Danish immigrant, Jacob Riis, who later became a famous journalist, photographer, and reformer, introduced the idea to the United States. The double-barred Cross of Lorraine became the seal's emblem in 1919.

In the 1920s, the selling of Christmas seals in the United States was taken over by the American Lung Association. By the time Einar Holboell died in 1927, he had received many honours, including knighthood. But what probably pleased him most was the progress and success in fighting tuberculosis.

Today, more than forty countries issue Christmas seals. In the United States, the American Lung Association sends Christmas seals to people through the mail and asks for a contribution. In Great Britain, many charities produce Christmas stamps to raise money. Thanks largely to the money raised from this effort, tuberculosis has become a rare disease.

Epiphany (see *Twelve Days of Christmas*)

Figgy Pudding. Anyone who has ever sung the British Christmas carol, "We Wish You A Merry Christmas," has probably wondered about the second verse, which says, "We all want some figgy pudding...so bring it right here!" This dessert was popular among British seamen during the nineteenth century.

Today, figgy pudding is largely unheard of in Great Britain. Instead, Christmas pudding is made to a recipe that is centuries old. Mrs. Beaton's has a recipe for figgy pudding which says that the pudding's ingredients include figs, breadcrumbs, treacle, eggs, and suet. The pudding is steamed in a pudding basin for four hours and served hot.

Frankincense and Myrrh, two of the gifts the three wise men gave the Baby Jesus, are pleasant-smelling substances made from the sap of certain trees found in Northeast Africa. At the time when Jesus was born, these types of incense were difficult to obtain and considered very valuable.

Good King Wenceslas (pronounced: Wen-suss-luss) is the name and subject of an old

Courtesy American Lung Association

English Christmas carol. This carol is based on a legend about King Wenceslas of Bohemia, a land that was once part of western Czechoslovakia. Wenceslas reigned during the tenth century and did much to strengthen people's belief in Christianity. He was known for his generosity and kindness. By the beginning of the next century, Wenceslas had become the patron saint of Bohemia.

The carol "Good King Wenceslas" tells the story of how one bitterly cold night on the Feast of St. Stephen (December 26), King Wenceslas looked out his castle window. Outside, the moonlight shone on the deep, crusty snow, and he saw a peasant gathering firewood. The king felt sorry for the poor man and called one of his pages to find out where the peasant lived. When the page replied that the peasant lived far away, the king called for some meat, wine, and firewood, which he decided he and the page would bring to the man's house.

The journey to the peasant's house was long, cold, and difficult in the deep snow. Finally, the page said that he was too cold to go any further. But King Wenceslas told the page that if he followed along in the king's footprints, he would feel warmer. The servant obeyed and, miraculously, heat seemed to come out of each of King Wenceslas's footsteps. The carol's lesson is, "Those that help the poor shall be helped as well."

Jesus, or Jesus Christ is the name that people call the Son of God, who is hon-

oured on Christmas. In the Bible, Mary is told that she will name her son, "Jesus." This is the Greek name for "Joshua," which means "Saviour" in Hebrew, the original language of the Bible. The name, "Christ," is a Greek word that means, "Messiah," or "Holy One."

Manger, the place where Mary placed the Baby Jesus upon his birth, is a trough or open box in which food for cattle, horses, or sheep is placed. It is probable that Mary's husband, Joseph, cleaned the manger and spread it with fresh hay, before laying his newborn son in it.

Noël is the French word for "Christmas." The Christmas carol "The First Noël"

© Ann Hagen Griffiths 1987/Omni-Photo Communications

Shepherds visit the Baby Jesus on the first Noel.

(sometimes spelled "Nowell") has made it a familiar word to English-speaking countries as well. "Noël" is derived from the Latin words for "birthday" ("Dies Natalis"), for it is on Christmas that people celebrate the Birth of Christ. In Italy, Christmas is called "Il Natale;" in Portugal and Brazil, "O Natal;" in Spanish-speaking countries, "La Navidad;" and in Wales, "Nadolig."

Swaddling clothes. In olden times, newborn babies were wrapped tightly in strips of linen or other cloth. This made them feel warm, secure, and protected. The word "swaddling" comes from an Old English word meaning "to wrap."

Twelve Days of Christmas. The twelve days from Christmas to Epiphany, on January 6, were once considered sacred.

In ancient Eastern Europe, Christians thought celebrating one's birthday—even the Birth of Christ—was unholy. For that reason, Eastern Christians used to celebrate Epiphany, which is also called "Little Christmas" and "Twelfth Day." Epiphany commemorates the three wise men's arrival in Bethlehem, which was a sign to all that Jesus was truly the Son of God.

Nothing invokes the spirit of the Christmas season more than stockings hung by the fireplace.

Yule is another name for the Christmas season of festivity and feasting. The word comes from ancient times, before Christ, when people in Northern Europe held their mid-winter festivals. "Yule" is thought to come from the ancient word for "wheel," which referred to the sun. This mid-winter "Yuletide" season was when people prayed to their gods for the sun and warmth to return to earth.

Yule Log Burning the Yule log is a tradition that was passed down from ancient Scandinavia. Though this custom was once practiced widely throughout Europe, it is now known mainly in Great Britain.

"Bringing in the Yule log" meant finding and cutting down a large tree on Christmas Eve. The log had to be very large, for it was supposed to burn throughout the twelve days of Christmas. Giant oak trees with large, twisted roots were often good choices.

Getting the log home was a group activity and especially fun for children. The log was tied up in a rope, and everyone who helped pull the log home was said to have good luck in the coming year. The log would be placed on the hearth, or fireplace, and lit with some of the kindling from last year's log.

Scraps from Yule logs were put away carefully each year after the holiday, to be taken out to light the next year's Yule log. In the meantime, people believed that the wood pieces would protect their home from fire and lightning during the year ahead.

Wassail (pronounced: WASS-el or was-SALE) means "to your health!" It is an ancient English toast that was usually said during festive celebrations. People would raise their glasses of wine, shout out "Wassail!" and then drink, as a sign of goodwill to each other.

"Wassail" is also a drink made from ale or wine, or both, and spiced with roasted apples and sugar. The bowl in which it is served is called a "wassail bowl."

"Wassailing" refers to the revelry that usually occurs while drinking from the wassail bowl.

THE STORY OF FATHER CHRISTMAS AND OTHER SPECIAL CHRISTMAS PEOPLE

Who has a long, white beard, wears a bright, red suit and stocking cap, and brings gifts and joy to children at Christmas? Why, Father Christmas, of course! All over the world, children of all ages look forward to his yearly visit, for Father Christmas, or "Santa Claus," as he is known in some countries, is everybody's special friend.

And yet Father Christmas is a mystery —a sort of magical mystery. After all, very few people (if any) have actually seen Father Christmas deliver gifts on Christmas Eve. He only visits homes once everyone is asleep.

Still, most people agree that Father Christmas rides through the sky on a sleigh pulled by reindeer, slips down the chimney (or enters the house in some other mysterious way, if there is no chimney), fills children's stockings or pillow cases with little gifts and goodies, and leaves bigger gifts around the Christmas tree.

Father Christmas is known to live at the North Pole, where he and his troop of merry elves work all year making gifts for good girls and boys. Throughout the year, Father Christmas receives many, many letters from children, who tell him what they would like for Christmas. Father Christmas does his best to give children what they want.

On Christmas Eve, he loads up his sleigh with sacks of toys and harnesses his team of flying reindeer to it. Then,

with a "Ho! Ho! Ho!", Father Christmas climbs into the sleigh and flies off into the night, delivering gifts to children around the world.

The next morning, the signs that Father Christmas has visited are usually

Illustration by Thomas Nast

New York Public Library/Picture Collection

Who Was Saint Nicholas?

Father Christmas is really another name for Saint Nicholas. This saint lived almost two thousand years ago in Asia Minor, which is now the country Turkey. He was not born a saint, but rather, just a simple, good boy named Nicholas.

When Nicholas grew up, he became a bishop and spread the word of Christ. At that time, Christianity was not accepted by most people, including the evil ruler of Asia Minor. Bishop Nicholas and his Christian followers were thrown in prison for their beliefs. But Nicholas was brave and helped encourage his fellow prisoners to be strong. Finally, after seven long years in prison, a new, kind ruler came to power and set Nicholas and the other Christians free.

The years that Nicholas had spent in prison had made him wiser, more understanding, and more willing than ever to help others. By the time he died, on December 6 in the year 343, there were many stories about his good deeds.

These tales were such fine examples of faith, courage, and kindness, that the memory of the good Bishop Nicholas lived on in people's hearts. Soon, he was declared a saint. As years passed, the legends about St. Nicholas grew. He became known as the Secret Gift-Bringer, as well as the Protector of Children.

clear: the biscuits left for him are eaten, he has left his gifts and perhaps a note for the children of the house, and *sometimes* it's even possible to see sleigh tracks on the roof!

But where did Father Christmas come from? How old is he? Has he always been magical? These are difficult questions, especially since no one was around when Father Christmas was born. Nevertheless, historians have found writings and tales that help provide the answers to these questions. Some of these stories are told in the following pages.

In olden days, people believed Saint Nicholas rode a white horse to deliver his presents.

New York Public Library/Picture Collection

THE SECRET GIFT-BRINGER

When St. Nicholas was a young man in Asia Minor, he heard about a merchant so poor that he thought he would have to sell his three lovely daughters into slavery. The eldest daughter wished to marry, but because she had no wealth to offer a husband, no man wanted her.

Nicholas knew the merchant would be too proud to accept any money as charity, so he came up with a secret plan to save the merchant and his daughters. Late one night, Nicholas wrapped three gold coins in a cloth and crept through the dark streets to the merchant's house. When he was sure that all were asleep, Nicholas tossed the little sack of coins into the house through an open window. Then he hurried back home.

When the merchant awoke the next morning, he could not believe his eyes: there, lying in the hearth, were three gold coins. He could not imagine who would have given him such a gift, so he believed it was from God. One gold coin was all the eldest daughter needed for a wedding offer, and she was soon married. The other two daughters were able to remain at home with their father.

But when it came time for the second daughter to marry, there was no money left. Again, Nicholas crept to the house and secretly tossed more gold coins in through the window. The merchant was amazed and grateful at finding more money. He accepted the gold as a gift from God, but now he was curious.

When the youngest daughter was ready to marry, Nicholas returned to the house once more. Quietly, he tossed the coins in through the window. But this time, the merchant had been waiting and watching. He jumped up and ran out the door.

"Stop! Wait!" the merchant called, and he ran until he caught up with Nicholas.

Nicholas begged the old man not to tell anyone of his deed. The merchant reluctantly obeyed and did not tell the secret, until he was about to die. Then he told the tale, and once it became known, the story spread throughout the land and established St. Nicholas as The Secret Gift-Bringer.

THE PROTECTOR OF CHILDREN

A young fisherman's son named Basil was walking along the beach one day when, suddenly, Arab pirates sprang out from hiding and kidnapped him. The pirates brought Basil to their land and made him a servant in the emperor's palace.

Meanwhile, Basil's parents did not know what had happened to their son. They cried and cried over their loss, and every day they prayed for Basil's safe return. A year passed, and Basil was still lost. On December 6, St. Nicholas Day, Basil's parents went to church and prayed extra hard for their son to come home.

That evening, the dogs began barking furiously outside Basil's house. The two parents went to see what was wrong—and then cried out in joy: there, at the gate in servant's clothing, was their son!

Basil told them how he had been kidnapped a year before. "But tonight," he said, "as I was serving the ruler's dinner, I suddenly felt myself being lifted into the sky. I turned around and saw I was staring right into the eyes of St. Nicholas."

Basil then had looked down and was startled to see that the earth was far below him.

"Don't be afraid," St. Nicholas had said, and Basil relaxed, knowing the good saint would protect him.

"Where are you taking me?" the young boy asked.

"I'm returning you to your parents,"

said St. Nicholas, "because they have prayed so hard for you to come home."

Basil and his family lived happily together for many years. The story of Basil's rescue was retold everywhere, and St. Nicholas became known as the Protector of Children.

New York Public Library/Picture Collection

ST. NICHOLAS COMES TO EUROPE

The tales and legends of St. Nicholas were passed on from generation to generation over the centuries that followed. St. Nicholas was so beloved that Russia and Greece adopted him as their patron (or protector) saint, and hundreds of churches throughout Europe were dedicated to him.

December 6, the Feast of St. Nicholas, was celebrated as the time when the saint would make his annual trip to earth.

Back then, people perceived St. Nicholas as a stately, bearded bishop who wore

© K. Reinhardt 1987/FPG Intl.

long, flowing robes and rode a white horse. On his head he wore a tall, pointed bishop's hat and he carried a staff as a symbol of his power and goodness. Children especially looked forward to his visit, for St. Nicholas was their protector and a gift-bringer as well.

On the eve of St. Nicholas Day, children would set hay and carrots out on the doorstep for the saint's white horse to eat, after his long trip down to earth from Heaven. It seemed only natural that St. Nicholas would give children something in return. At first, the saint left little presents hidden inside carrots and cabbages. In time, St. Nicholas brought different kinds of gifts, and he left them in children's shoes or stockings placed by the hearth.

But even in those days, St. Nicholas was a mystery. No one could ever say for sure exactly how the saint appeared on the eve of his feast day, because no one ever saw him.

In Belgium, St. Nicholas was thought to carry a big book so he could write down the names of the good children who deserved gifts. In Holland, St. Nicholas delivered presents to the good children, while a mean-looking servant called "Black Peter" carried birch rods for the naughty ones. Black Peter also carried a big, heavy bag for carrying away extremely bad children. In Germany, a bearded man dressed all in fur, named "Fur Nicholas," carried a bag of coal with him to give to bad children.

The thought of Black Peter or Fur Nicholas would scare children into being good. But no one ever feared St. Nicholas—he rewarded the good children but never punished the bad.

New York Public Library/Picture Collection

ST. NICHOLAS AS FATHER CHRISTMAS

Once Christianity had been established throughout Europe, people began to have religious differences. Eventually, Christians split into two main groups: the Catholics (the older group) and the Protestants.

Protestants in Great Britain, France, and Germany stopped worshipping saints altogether—including St. Nicholas. But it was impossible to forget this good saint and protector of children. Instead, they gave St. Nicholas a new name: "Father Christmas," or "Père Nöel" in French. In parts of Switzerland and West Germany, St. Nicholas came to be called simply, "Ni-

kolaus," or the "Weihnachtsman," which means "the Christmas man."

In some countries, Father Christmas continued to come on December 6, the Feast of St. Nicholas, while in others, he arrived on Christmas Eve. Otherwise, the new "Father Christmas" remained very much like the good St. Nicholas everyone had always known. Father Christmas still dressed in bishop's robes and rode a tall, white horse, and he continued to bring gifts to all good children.

Over time, Father Christmas changed his style and appearance. But today, Father Christmas and America's Santa Claus are one and the same "jolly old elf"—and he is loved just as much whatever his name and whatever his costume.

Gift-Bringers From Around The World

Many children around the world await different gift-bringers. Still, these gift-bringers are just as magical, mysterious, and well-loved as St. Nicholas, Father Christmas, and Santa Claus.

THE BEFANA OF ITALY

The Befana is a mysterious, old woman who visits the world on the eve of Epiphany. Some people call Befana a witch, for she has magical powers to reward good children and punish the bad ones. But throughout Italy, the Befana is known for her kind heart and for bringing goodies and gifts to children.

In some areas of Italy, the Befana announces her approach to each house by ringing a bell. That is her signal for children to go to bed, for the Befana will not enter a house until all are asleep. Many children hang stockings by the window for the Befana to fill with sweets, fruits, and gifts.

The Befana, known as the "Baboushka" in Russia, is said to have passed up the opportunity to join the three wise men on their search for the Baby Jesus. Because she never found the Christ Child herself and was not able to give him a gift, the Befana began secretly bringing gifts to other children instead. The Befana makes her trip each year on January 5. (For the complete story, see page 124.)

JULTOMTE: THE SWEDISH CHRISTMAS ELF

In olden days, when most people in Sweden lived on farms, people believed that goblins, trolls, and other strange creatures, called "jultomten" (pronounced: yool-TOME-Ten), lived in the nooks and crannies of every home. These creatures caused much mischief, especially in the cold, dark month of December. Families would try to get along with these jultomten as best they could. They would leave them porridge to eat and keep the house as clean as possible.

Over the years, the jultomten have mostly disappeared. Perhaps they are hiding in the forest and countryside. Now Swedish children are visited by the good and jolly gift-bringer, the "Jultomte," the Swedish name for Father Christmas.

In Sweden, the Jultomte does things a little differently from other countries. There, he comes on foot and carries his bag of toys and goodies on his back. The Jultomte arrives early on Christmas Eve, while the children are still awake and eagerly awaiting his arrival.

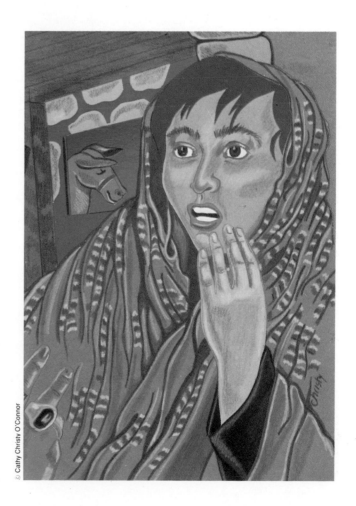

© Cathy Christy O'Connor

"Las Posadas," the traditional Spanish procession, reenacts the night Jesus was born.

As this painting by N.C. Wyeth illustrates, Father Christmas visits homes all over the world with his sack of toys.

THE THREE KINGS OF MEXICO

The Christmas season in Mexico and other Spanish-speaking countries begins with colourful parades and candlelight processions in the evening. The processions, called "Las Posadas," act out the night Jesus was born. Children dress up as angels, shepherds, Mary, Joseph, and the Three Kings.

Festivities continue through Epiphany, January 6, which is also called "Three Kings Day." This was the day the Three Kings (or wise men) found Jesus lying in the manger in Bethlehem. On Epiphany Eve, the Three Kings come down to earth, dressed in their long, royal robes and crowns. Before going to sleep on that night, children set their shoes out on the doorstep so the Three Kings may fill them with gifts and sweets as they pass.

THE "LITTLE CHRIST CHILD" OF WEST GERMANY

The "Christkindl," (pronounced: Krisst KIN-del) or "Little Christ Child" looks like a young angel, dressed in white robes with golden wings and a crown. He flies down to earth on Christmas Eve, and puts gifts for children under the Christmas tree.

Today, "Kriss Kringle" is another name for Father Christmas. The name came from the Germans, who brought their "Christkindl" with them when they came to the United States. Their American neighbours, who did not understand German, thought they were saying, "Kriss Kringle." In time, German-American children adopted the American Father Christmas as their Christmas gift-bearer, and Kriss Kringle and Father Christmas became one and the same.

YOU CAN BE A GIFT-BRINGER TOO

To be a gift-bringer in your own family or circle of friends, it's not necessary to dress up as one. All you need are the kind and generous thoughts of giving joy to others, which all gift-bringers share.

Gifts do not have to be as fancy or expensive as the gifts the three wise men gave Jesus. Instead, think of the story of the little Mexican boy, who gave the Baby Jesus a simple poinsettia.

The following section will give you ideas on how to make your own gifts, or how to add a personal touch to something you have bought. Remember: What makes each gift valuable is the thought and love behind it.

Gift giving, inspired by the first Christmas when the three wise men brought gold, frankincense, and myrrh to the Christ Child, has become one of the hallmarks of the Christmas season.

Part II

HOLIDAY CRAFTS AND RECIPES

Richard Waldmann

HOW TO MAKE CHRISTMAS CARDS

Everyone likes to receive Christmas cards—and receiving a handmade card is even better. It means that someone has taken a little extra time, thought, and imagination to send you holiday greetings. And that's what Christmas is all about.

There is no one way to make a Christmas card; what your card looks like depends on what you like doing best. This section explains how to make six different types of cards:

Christmas drawings
Christmas card cut-outs from paper
Christmas card cut-outs from other material
Christmas sponge patterns
Christmas card cut-outs from magazines
Christmas photographs

These ideas are meant to help you decide what kind of card you wish to make. Feel free to use your imagination, however, to make your card unique.

What You Need To Make Your Christmas Card:

- Coloured Card. This paper is both sturdy and colourful. It is thick enough to support glued-on shapes, and if you draw on it with coloured markers, the ink will not leak through to the other side.

- Scissors. Scissors with rounded ends, which are small, light, and easy to handle, are the best kind of scissors to use. If you must use a larger, sharper pair, make sure you have your parents' permission.

- Glue. Use regular rubber cement to stick things, according to the suggestions outlined below and on the next page.

A WORD ABOUT GLUES

White glue usually comes in a small, plastic bottle. It's easy to use and sticks well. However, once you have glued something, like a picture, onto your paper, it is almost impos-

Professionally made cards often can provide inspiration for your own unique Christmas card designs.

GLUING TIPS

1. Apply the glue evenly to whatever you wish to attach to your card. The most important areas to cover are the corners. You may want to take your finger and smear a little of the glue smoothly onto the corners and along the sides.

2. With rubber cement, wipe the excess from the brush on the side of the container before applying the brush to the item being glued on.

3. Whether using rubber cement or white glue, never apply it heavily or in big globs—the result will be messy and lumpy if you do.

4. For extra-small cut-outs or corners, it sometimes helps to put a small mound of adhesive on an extra piece of paper or cardboard. Lightly dip your finger into it and dab it onto your cut-out or corner.

GLITTER TIPS

Trimming your card with glitter is easy and it adds a bit of sparkle as well. *Make sure your work space is covered with newspaper.* Here's what you do:

1. Decide where you want the glitter to go—around the edges, in a special design, or in a particular place.

2. Brush the rubber cement or put the white glue onto the place where you want the glitter.

3. Quickly, before the glue dries, pour the glitter over it on the page. Put on lots of glitter so that every spot is covered.

4. Let the card dry for a few minutes.

5. Pick up the finished card and shake the extra glitter onto the newspaper. You can save that extra glitter for later projects.

Tony Cenicola

White glue is easy to dab on but if you make a mistake it is harder to wipe off than rubber cement.

sible to move it without tearing the paper or leaving glue marks.

Rubber cement usually comes in a jar with a brush attached to the top. It sticks as well as white glue, but rubber cement allows you to make mistakes. In most cases, you can pull off whatever you have glued on without tearing it. Be sure to pull it off gently, though. Once you have pulled it off, simply rub off the dried glue. Then apply some fresh rubber cement, and stick the item back on the card.

How To Begin Your Christmas Card:

1. Take a piece of coloured card. Notice that it has two long sides and two short sides.

2. Bring the two short sides together at one end. Flatten the other end down to make a fold. We'll call this Fold 1.

3. Now bring the two short sides together again, and make another fold. We'll call this Fold 2.

4. With your scissors, cut along Fold 2.

5. You should now have two equal-sized cards, ready to decorate.

Fold the two short sides of the coloured card together. Then bring the two short sides together again.

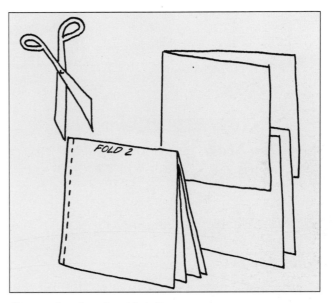

Next, cut the coloured card in half.

"But What Should It Look Like?"—Ideas For Your Cards

- Think of the friend or relative who will receive your card. What do you and that person do together? What does that person like? Did you have an adventure together? Did you do something wonderful together *last* Christmas that you hope this special person will remember, too? Use your memories to help give you an idea.

- Look all around you for Christmas ideas. Is your town dressed up in garlands and col-oured lights? Are there Christmas trees in your neighbours' windows and wreaths on their doors? Those make pretty pictures.

- Christmas books and magazines are also full of fun pictures. Use them for ideas.

Below are six different sorts of Christmas cards to make. Choose the one that will be the most fun for you to create. If you do not have two plain, equal-sized cards ready to decorate, go back to *"What You Need To Make Your Christmas Card"* and *"How To Begin Your Christmas Card"* and follow those instructions. Then continue your card-making with the directions below.

CHRISTMAS DRAWINGS

What You Need: pencil, coloured felt tips, coloured pencils or paint, white or light-coloured paper.

Optional: glitter and glue.

What You Do:

1. In pencil, draw a Christmas picture on the front of your card. (It's best not to colour your picture until the written message is finished, too.)

2. Once your picture is right, write a message in pencil on the inside of the card. For variety, you can start the message on the outside cover and finish it on the inside.

3. Go over your message in coloured felt tip or pencil.

4. Now colour your card.

Optional:

5. Trim your card with glitter.

CHRISTMAS CARD CUT-OUTS FROM PAPER

What You Need: pencil, coloured card or Christmas wrapping paper, scissors, glue, coloured felt tips or pencils.

Optional: glitter.

What You Do:

1. Using a pencil, draw a Christmas shape, such as a candle, star, Christmas tree, or Christmas tree ornament, on a clean piece of coloured card. If you have trouble drawing, perhaps you can find an appropriate shape on Christmas wrapping paper and cut that out.

2. Carefully cut the shape out with scissors.

3. Glue it onto the front of your card.

4. Write your Christmas message on your card in pencil first, then go over it in coloured felt tip or pencil.

Optional:

5. Trim your card with glitter.

CHRISTMAS CARD CUT-OUTS FROM OTHER MATERIAL

What You Need: small pieces of pretty material—cotton, felt, or practically any left-over material in a sewing basket (*and* permission to use the material), pencil, scissors, glue, coloured felt tips.

Optional: glitter, cotton wool, ribbon.

What You Do:

1. With a pencil, draw a simple Christmas shape—a candle, star, Christmas tree, or Christmas tree ornament on your piece of material.

2. Carefully cut out the pattern from the material.

3. Decide where you want the cut-out to go on your card, and then glue it in place.

4. With a pencil, write your Christmas message on your card. Go over the message with a coloured felt tip or pencil.

Optional:

5. Decorate your card with glitter, different small pieces of material, ribbon, or even bits of cotton wool for a snow effect.

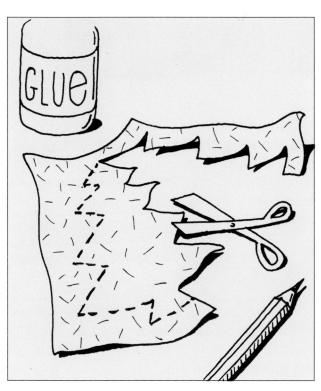

Cut your favourite Christmas shape from a pretty piece of fabric.

Glue the shape to your card and add a simple message.

© Christopher Bain 1988

Tony Cenicola

Dip your sponge piece in paint and lightly press it to the paper. You can repeat the pattern many times.

CHRISTMAS SPONGE PATTERNS

What You Need: a small sponge, scissors, poster paints, extra paper (for practice prints).

What You Do:

1. Wet the sponge, then squeeze out extra water. (Damp sponges are easier to cut than dry ones.)

2. From the sponge, cut out a single Christmas shape—such as a candle, Christmas tree, or Christmas tree ornament. You could also simply cut out small circles or triangles to make a pretty design on your card.

3. Dip one side of the sponge cut-out into paint.

4. Make a test print with the sponge cut-out on an extra piece of paper. You may need to use more paint to make a heavier print, or less paint to make it lighter.

5. Once you have the right amount of paint on your sponge cut-out, press it against the paper to make a print or design onto your Christmas card.

6. Make as many prints on your card as you wish, but save room for your message and your name.

7. Print your Christmas message in pencil, then go over it in coloured felt tip or pencil.